# A CRICKET

*in the* Telephone

(*At* Sunset)

*Poems from*

*The Fessenden Review*

MHO & MHO WORKS

*1999*

A CRICKET
IN THE TELEPHONE
(AT SUNSET)

*Poems from*
*The Fessenden Review*

This book is published by Mho & Mho Works, San Diego, California.
Book design by Jennifer West.
Typeset in Mrs. Eaves and Meta.

For a free catalogue of other books offered by Mho & Mho Works,
write to Box 33135, San Diego, California 92163.

Library of Congress Cataloging-in-Publication Data

A cricket in the telephone (at sunset):
poems from The Fessenden Review / edited by Lolita Lark,
introduction by Lorenzo W. Milam.
    p. cm
ISBN 0-917320-14-X.  (hardback: alk. paper).
ISBN 0-917320-13-1 (pbk.: alk. paper).

    1. Poetry, Modern— 20th Century.   I. Lark, Lolita,
1940—
II. Title: Fessenden review
IN PROCESS
811' .5408—dc2                98-37182
                                CIP


1 2 3 4 5 6 7 8 9 10 J Q K A

## OTHER BOOKS BY
## OUR CONTRIBUTORS

A. W. Allworthy
The Petition Against God*
*(1975)*

Carlos Amantea
The Lourdes of Arizona*
*(1989)*

The Blob that Ate Oaxaca*
*(1992)*

Douglas Cruickshank
Swallowing
The Rototiller
*(1999)**

Lolita Lark
Lolita on Lolita:
A Transgenerational
Approach to Nabokov
*(Forthcoming)*

L. W. Milam
Under a Bed of Poses:
A Novel
*(1959)*

The Myrkin Papers
*(1969)*

Sex & Broadcasting*
*(1974)*

The Cripple Liberation Front
Marching Band Blues*
*(1984)*

The Radio Papers*
*(1986)*

Crip Zen*
*(1993)*

L. W. Milam & Jon Gallant
Gringolandia:
A Guide for Puzzled Mexicans*
*(1997)*

Ignacio Schwartz
Rock Gardening in
the Ukraine,
*(Forthcoming)*

*Available from Mho & Mho Works

# TABLE OF CONTENTS

*Introduction:* The Noisiest Book
Review in the Known World
Lorenzo W. Milam

17. A Cricket in the Telephone (At Sunset)
Ignacio Schwartz

19. Love & The Flowers
Jeremy D. Colon

20. Tootie-Fruit ME & Ass-Grasp LA
Brook Morris, Jr

22. The Battle at Little Bull Run
T. F. Bierly

25. Credo
Aquiles Nazoa
Translation by Carlos Amantea
and Renato Valenzuela

27. The Vivisection Mambo
P. J. Weise

29. The Ladies of the School
Lolita Lark

30. Saint Peter got Smashed
Pater Müller

32. A Story (A Wonderful Story)
Charles Wing Krafft

34. Fly Love Poem
Leslie Seamans

36. Casida de la Muchacha Dorada
*Federico García-Lorca*
*Translation by Carlos Amantea*

38. La Mano de Onan se Queja
*Manuel del Cabra*
*Translation by Carlos Amantea*
*and Renato Valenzuela*

42. Eulogy on the Death of Dickie Dickinson
(Who Weighed in at 335 Pounds)
*G. J. Fogerty*

44. The Stars ® Us
*Peter Dodge*

47. Moon Dog Song
*Jeremy D. Colon*

49. Song to SuppHose
*P. V. Astor, III*

51. The Return of Der Führer
*Jeremy W. Torg*

54. Jesus Under Water
*Al Hefid*

56. Did You See? She Had Flowers up Her Nose.
*Emma St. James*

57. Loos
*Edna J. Lacey*

58. Song of the Forget-Me-Not
*Cynthia Weiss*

60. Sing Ho! To the New Keyboard
*A. W. Allworthy*

61. *Dedication*: January 1940
*Roy Fuller*

# THE NOISIEST BOOK REVIEW
## IN THE KNOWN WORLD

For almost five years, *The Fessenden Review* served as
America's Literary Grouch. It not only entertained its
subscribers and those of us who put it together but—
apparently—other media people as well. It was the subject
of articles by writers at *The San Francisco Chronicle,
The Washington Post, The Los Angeles Times, Library Journal,* and
by interview on *National Public Radio,* among others.

All this came about because Douglas Cruickshank and I
decided to put together a book review magazine that showed
a bit of life. The Augean stables of American literature
smelled funny to us—and we thought it worthwhile to try to
clean them up a bit.

We also wanted to honor (and imitate) the early masters
of The Tart School of Review—H. L. Mencken, from his
*Smart Set* days; Virginia Woolf, who wrote for so many years
for *The London Times Literary Supplement*; and the superb
literary critics of the 50's and 60's appearing in *The New
Statesman, The London Observer, The Manchester Guardian,* and
Canada's *Saturday Night Magazine.*

It was our belief that most Americans had never been
exposed to righteous, pithy, critical overviews of the book
publishing world. We wanted to stir the pot of American
letters, to make writing about books more than back-
ground noise.

At first, it was hard to find writers for the magazine—those
who were free of the stylistic tics that infested *Publishers
Weekly, Kirkus,* and *The New York Times* as well as the book
sections of the daily and weekly newspapers and news mag-
azines. We convinced some of our more literate friends to
review for us, but, ultimately, our best source for good
writing turned out to be the fans of *TFR*.

If a reader sent us a letter of love, or one of complaint, and if the writing was half literate—we dragooned him or her into going to work for us (at $10 a shot). This system of literary feedback gave us some brilliant, new, and cranky writers. We also created a stable of fake names so that people would think we had a vast staff awaiting our assignments: Ignacio Schwartz, Jeremy Colon, Wanda Felix, Carlos Amantea, T.F. Bierly, A.W. Allworthy, Ángel Pérez, Gilo Coatimundi, G. J. Fogerty, and, my personal favorite, P. P. McFeelie. All of them were born in those heady days, and many have since gone on to more rewarding if less onerous tasks.

During its short, pithy life, *TFR* received thousands of books for review. We tried to take note of as many as possible, giving equal time to the famous and the not-so-famous, the great, the good, and the totally grim. We wanted to give all the kindness of being noticed—even if it meant frying their asses. That applied in spades to the books of verse that came our way. "We get anywhere between ten and twenty poetry books a week," we wrote in one of the early issues. "We find that most of the writers have been perverted by the doggerel that appears in *The Atlantic, The New Yorker,* and the 'little magazines' like *The Virginia Quarterly Review, The Kenyon Review, The Southern Review,* and their ilk."[1]

"What we want to do is to free American verse from the steely grip of the establishment poets, who—as far as we can figure, given their style—might as well be writing ad copy for Frito-Lay, McDonald's, or Smuckers. Those of us who grew up on Yeats or Eliot or e. e. cummings or Emily Dickinson feel that repetition, finely-honed rhythms, and a gentle turning of English can transform words, create a sweet magic, build joy out of what is, after all, nothing:

> *The woods decay, the woods decay and fall,*
> *The vapours weep their burthen to the ground,*
> *Man comes and tills the field and lies beneath,*
> *And after many a summer dies the swan.*

"It would be hard to find any more noble statement of simple life and simple death, the death of all of us (bird, beast, man alike); ideas set in majestic iambs, with a gracious symbolism, and the surprise of a final line that certainly must have been inspired by the gods."[2]

❧

Our caustic squibs got us many kind letters and comments. Max Lerner said, "The reviews break all conventions and are the stuff of life." Herbert Gold said, "I enjoy your quirky take on things—although you don't seem to review my books." Michael Parrish, editor of *The Los Angeles Times Magazine* said, "We love *The Fessenden Review*." And Lily Pond of *Yellow Silk* said "Yikes!" Norman Mailer—of all people—said, laconically, "It's worth having around."[3]

It was great fun while it lasted. We knew we had thousands of loyal readers, but what made it so enjoyable for us is the thing that finally did us in: the lack of advertisers or a university sponsor.

We knew our time was drawing nigh (we had to borrow money to put out the last issue), but, even so, we comforted ourselves by thinking of the other great American literary magazines that had gone out of business in this century: *Spicy-Adventure Stories, Foreign Legion Adventures, Rangeland Romances, Gang World, Wild West Weekly, Pep Stories, Weird Tales,* and *Racketeer Magazine.*

The last issue of *TFR* came out as fat and beautiful and funny as all its predecessors, deliciously designed by Cruickshank. There were almost ninety reviews and excerpts from books, twenty or so letters from readers,[4] and several poems. There were more than seventy photographs and drawings taken from the books that were raining down on us: a 1920s bus marked "Hibbing Public Library Service;" a lone, wide-eyed boy on a hilltop in Beirut, with smoke billowing up behind him; family shots by Nicholas Nixon; photos of Jim and Tammy Bakker, Elvis Presley, the Duke and Duchess of Windsor, Mark Twain, Oscar Wilde—and a full-page, glorious, unsmiling Queen Victoria.

There was a silhouette from the 18th century, and an early
advertisement for Apex radios. There was a convoluted
wood engraving by Peter Bruegel the Elder, a steam iron
(a steam iron!) melted by the folks at *Consumer Reports,* and
a several delicious animal pictures (Cruickshank was nuts
about fat dogs, pigs, giraffes, toads and penguins. In fact,
he has told close friends that he knows—he doesn't think,
he knows—that he's a penguin).

The books reviewed in the last issue were typical:
*Memories of Amnesia, The Life and Letters of Tofu Roshi, The Making
of the African Queen, The Boz, The Windsor Style, Loving Little Egypt,
Fort Bragg* and *Other Points South, Collecting Antique Marbles,
Dangerous Dossiers, The Pocket Doctor, A Journey to the Far Canine
Range, The Paintings of William Burroughs, The Easy Money Diet,
Radio Manufacturers of the 1920s, In Flanders Fields, Memoirs of
My Nervous Illness*—and one of my favorite obscure books
of all times, from Harvard University Press, Alexander A.
Potebnja's *Psycholinguistic Theory of Literature: A Metacritical
Inquiry.*[5]

The cover of the last issue was pure Fessenden: it showed
a Mexican *lucha libre* star, in full regalia. Along the spine
we listed

Italo Calvino
Barbara Tuchman
Eudora Welty
Primo Levi
Jean Genet
Günter Grass
Ivan Illich
Nadine Gordimer
John Lilly
Nancy Mitford
Freeman Dyson
Muriel Spark
Charles Reich
Umberto Eco
Lawrence Durrell

Were any of their books reviewed, or even mentioned,
inside the magazine? Of course not. We were just, as
usual—there on the funeral pyre—being our usual literary
smart-alecky selves.[6]

*The Fessenden Review* is now a stack of papers over there in the far corner of the closet, collecting dust and rat shit, reminding me of Hexagram Four in the *I Ching*—Mîng ("Youthful Folly").[7] Cruickshank and I (and Felix, McFeelie, Amantea, and Lark) thought that, operating on our own, we could root the turnips out of the cellars, get some bats up into the belfry, where they belong. For a brief moment there, we were in the same stratosphere as *PW, The New York Review of Books, Booklist, Library Journal, Choice,* and *Kirkus*—and we loved it. We wanted not only to move our readers, but give inspiration to those nut cases who create the more than 60,000 new titles that come off the presses each year.

Despite our crabbiness, I like to think that those of us who produced *The Fessenden Review* were true innocents, offering something to other innocents trying to be heard: saying that the time and trouble they took to produce a book was worth it, saying that there was one magazine that would give them a chance, take the time to respond—to respond to banality with snappishness, to hope with hope, and to high art with artful and worthy praise.

We (and they) could ask no less.


*Lorenzo W. Milam*
January 1999


NOTE:
Because of the economics of the cathode ray tube vs. paper,
electronic imagery vs. ink printing, the World Wide Web vs. web press,
parts of *The Fessenden Review* have been reactivated at
**http://www.ralphmag.org**
The only difference is that we have chosen to rechristen it as
*The Review of Arts, Literature, Politics, and the Humanities.*
Or, more succinctly, RALPH.

# FOOTNOTES

1. Our especial bugbear was what Jimmy Merrill called "the 40's formalism," represented by Howard Moss, Louis Simpson, Richard Howard, Richard Wilbur, John Hollander, and Robert Penn Warren. Of the latter, in a review of one of his anthologies, we suggested that he "...might consider retirement to the pleasant reaches of Disneyland, to a prestigious Chair ('The Mickey Mouse Chair of Poetry' for example)—so that American poetry could move on to artistry of a more vigorous, vibrant, and virile nature."

2. Ours, however, was not merely a seek-and-destroy mission. Along with our terse criticisms, we felt it our duty to publish worthwhile poetry. During the lifetime of the magazine, we printed or reprinted over 300 poems—many of them drawn from books sent to us, or individual submissions that came in the mail. These poems are the ostensible subject of this book.

3. The best review of them all was by Gary Indiana, who wrote in the Village Voice: "[It's] like a *New York Review of Books* for the living—wildly eclectic, suggestive even when it's murky, unafraid to offer a one-sentence review of a new translation of Camus's *The Stranger*, ('It makes no difference') or a quick puncture to the unseemly literary fecundity of May Sarton ('As far as we can figure it, Ms. Sarton either owns 25 percent of the preferred stock in W. W. Norton Co., or has some terrible secret she's holding over the Chairman of the Board.') Unlike *The New York Review*, this isn't a magazine by people who have had their hands in each other's pockets for so long that the reader need only scan the cover to see whose balls are being stroked inside. Part of *The Fessenden Review's* charm is the opacity of its agenda and its willingness to trash established mediocrity, praise the heretofore unknown, and run lengthy pieces full of quirky, unexpected insight and unsentimentalized honesty (like Mark O'Brien's first-person account of a disabled writer's efforts to interview Stephen Hawking)— in other words, the qualities that made *The New York Review* the best literary magazine in America."

4. Including one from a prisoner that said, "If I were published, I would consider it an honor to be panned in *TFR!*" Another came in from Kevin Kelly, of *The Whole Earth Review*: "Apparently it's *de rigueur* among all hot shot editors to have their blurb appear on the back page of The Fessenden Review. Not to be out-classed by my ambitious peers, I forthwith submit my tribute... 'The choicest place in the universe to find the most extraordinary reviews or ordinary (or worse) books. Via the sharp wit and bad attitude of *Fessenden* reviewers, I derive literary pleasure from books I'd otherwise rather compost than read.' "

5. Our review began "Potebnja was another one of those dratted nineteenth century Ukrainian café intellectuals whose mother refused to give him a name we could cotton to—or even spell."

6. To be even more smart alecky, we snuck in a few names that we had made up—names that sounded literary, but that were strictly whole-cloth: Isabel Luis Corazón, Anwak Fayoumi, P. J. Weise, Jorge Amado, Lolita Lark, Laura Huxley. Names to test people. Just to make sure they were paying attention.

7. "Youthful folly has success.
   It is not I who seek the young fool;
   The young fool seeks me.
   If he importunes, I give him no information.
   Perseverance furthers...
   In punishing folly
   It does not further one
   To commit transgressions."

# A CRICKET

*in the* Telephone

(*At* Sunset)

*Poems from*

*The Fessenden Review*

Edited by
*Lolita Lark*

With an Introduction by
*Lorenzo W. Milam*

MHO & MHO WORKS

*1999*

## A Cricket in the Telephone
### (at Sunset)

I could hear the border guards cheering
So it must have been before midnight;
A mosquito (*Stegomyia,* not *Anopheles*)
Was singing love songs in my ear.
You called to tell me something about
Mothers, or was it Mother, or was it me?
Microscopic electrons from microspace
Turned your voice to fruit salad.

I found myself thinking of mosquitoes,
(*Stegomyia,* not *Anopheles*)
And your great gorgeous thighs,
While somewhere inside
(The telephone, not you),
There was a chirping noise:
"Cheer-UP, Cheer-UP" it said.

The Buddhists tell us that Truth
Lies between the space between thoughts
And the stars, perhaps just this side of
*Andromeda* (or is it *Anopheles*?)

I find that if I think too much
On you and on my love for you,
The stars begin to talk to me,
Talk to me of Standard and Poors, and
Sweet Virginia peppermint pie, and
The decline of the Roman Empire, and

The new, complete, unabridged
*Memoirs of Jacques Casanova...* and, and
You half-hidden under the bedcovers,
    Mussed, peering at me.

            Later that night,
        Or was it the next day?
        You called back to say
        I was driving you potty
    (That was the word you used).
It was, you said, not your fault,
But, you said, my restless brain,
    The endless talk, talk, talk,
My restless fingers all over you
        Making you quite daft.
    That was the word you used.

                I asked
            If you could hear
            The crickets
        In the telephone
            (At sunset)?

—*Ignacio Schwartz*

## Love & the Flowers

Darling there is a worm in your flower
Among other things
And the sight of his gray face
Brings to mind the night

On a slow trolley
Beating down the tracks to Madrid
I saw a young man of wit and determination
Eating a wild red carnation.

Love and the flowers
And such a past is not too easy to forget;
Sometimes I think it gets too soon too late—
And sometimes I think of the terrible dark
     space
Lying between stars and petals.

There is a worm in your flower darling
And your mind like mine
Is growing tattered
And the flakes of night come drifting down
And I do love your poor old bones too dearly.

Love and the flowers
And age drawing on like a shawl.
It seems to me the days are coming shorter
And the sun takes such a crooked path
Down to the crooked sea.

—*Jeremy D. Colon*

## Tootie-Fruit ME & Ass-Grasp LA

All the babies were behaving as if they were moons,
Crawling out of seashells, stuffed blind as turkeys.
They smelt of the flat fever of love, with chancres
    Born of Vanilla Bean WY, or Sewer Stop AK.

We brought them up to believe in wombats fed on
Shroud thighs, with crowds of crying turtles, &
Peasant armies of hymn-singing, drug-ridden geckos,
    All singing "Om Mani Padme Hum, Om Mani."

In our town we have widows watering their proud
Buttocks, witches who would let us off, without
Consultation, in Pork Chop MO or Dog Stool IL...
All twelve of us at the depot with our bent ankles
    And a blind (and healthy) love for sweet waffles.

They say we were part of the Breadfruit Conspiracy
Out of Tootie Fruit ME because we petitioned the gods
(Gods with marble eyes) to stop smelling up Newton's
Third Law of Generations with love. We begged them
    To leave us singing "Om Mani Padme Hum,
    Om Mani."

In conclusion, I should like to report that our brains
Are now pickled & dried with love, & are thus
    weighted
In units of filial darkness. Our watches separate
    time
From space (in planetary feet) & thus put us on the
Very last train to Bugger Bean OH or Assgrasp LA,
    All singing "Om Mani Padme Hum, Om Mani."

                    *—Brook Morris, Jr.*

## The Battle at Little Bull Run

My family laughs before the fire
Serves distress from the carcass
Of smoked duck Mandarin sauce.
They dissolve all wounds in demitasse
And leaded decanters of Southern Comfort
Served neat, with brandied berries.

My family eats love for dessert
Topped with nutmeats and cherries.
When asked, they smile out of the past
And crush the small rebellions we bring
From school: crayon drawings of skulls,
Paper dolls with scrofula, dead pups.

My family sleeps on love like a drug:
At night they hear the wind through
The pikestaffs, songs of damned boys
Who lost their lives on the fields
At Sharpsburg.

       In early morning,
Before the angels' great stone fire,
They wipe away our tears, roast us
Over hot coals. Our joy leaks
Down our cheeks like fat, hissing
And spattering on the coals.

*—T. F. Bierly*

# CREDO

Creo en Pablo Neruda, todopoderoso
creador del cielo y de la tierra
Creo en Charlie Chaplin
Hijo de las violetas y los ratones
que fue crucificado, muerto y sepultado
por el tiempo, pero que cada dia resucita
en el corazón de los hombres
Creo en el amor y el arte
como vias hacia el disfrute de la vida perdurable
Creo en los grillos
que pueblan la noche de mágicos cristales
Creo en el amolador
que vive de fabricar estrellas con su rueda maravillosa
Creo en la cualidad aérea del hombre
configurado en el recuerdo
de Isadora Duncan
abatiéndose como una purísima paloma herida
        bajo el cielo del Mediterraneo
Creo en las monedas de chocolate
que atesoro bajo la almohada de mi niñez
Creo en la fábula de Orfeo
Creo en el sortilegio de la musica
yo que en las horas de mi angustia vi
al conjuro de la pavana de Fauré
salir liberada y radiante
a la dulce Euridice del infierno de mi alma
Creo en Rainer Maria Rilke
héroe de la lucha del hombre

por la belleza, que sacrifico su vida
al acto de cortar una rosa por una mujer
Creo en las rosas que brotarón del cadaver adolescente
    de Ofelia
Creo en el llanto silencioso de Aquiles
        frente al mar
Creo en un barco esbelto y distantísimo
que salió hace un siglo al encuentro de la aurora
Su capitán Lord Byron
al cinto las espadas de los arcangeles
y junto a sus sienes
el resplandor de las estrellas
Creo en el perro de Ulises
y en el gato risueño
de Alicia en el País de las Maravillas
En el loro de Robinson Crusoe
En los ratoncitos que tirarón
el carro de la Cenicienta
En Beralfiro, el caballo de Rolando
y en las abejas que labran
su colmena dentro de corazón de Martín Tinajero
Creo en la amistad
como en el invento mas bello del hombre
Creo en los poderes creadores del pueblo
Y creo en mí
puesto que se que hay alguien
que me ama

—*Aquiles Nazoa*

## CREDO

I believe in Pablo Neruda, almighty creator of heaven
    and earth
I believe in Charlie Chaplin
Son of violets and mice
Who was crucified, died, and laid in the grave by
    his era,
but who each day is revived in the hearts of men
I believe in love and art
As ways to find joy in the hardness of life
I believe in the crickets that people the magic
    crystal night
I believe in the miller who lives to create stars
    with his marvelous wheel
I believe in the highest gifts of humanity
    configured in the memory
of Isadora Duncan
brought down like a pure, wounded dove under
    the Mediterranean sky
I believe in the chocolate coins that I hide under
    the rug of my childhood
I believe in the legend of Orpheus
I believe in the sorcery of music that in the hours
    of my anguish I saw
under the spell of Fauré's *Pavanne*
leaving sweet Euridice liberated and radiant
    from the inferno of my soul
I believe in Rainer Maria Rilke

hero of humanity's struggle
for beauty, who sacrificed his life
while picking a rose for a lady
I believe in the roses that burst forth
from the adolescent corpse of Ophelia
I believe in the silence of Achilles weeping
      before the sea
I believe in a small and distant ship
that left a century ago to meet the sun
Its captain Lord Byron
in his belt the archangels' swords
and around his temples
the splendor of the stars
I believe in Ulysses' dog
and in Alice's cat
smiling in Wonderland
In Robinson Crusoe's parrot
In the mice that pulled
Cinderella's carriage
In Berylfire, Roland's horse
and in the bees that build their hive in the heart
      of Martín Tinajero
I believe in kindness
as the most lovely creation of mankind
I believe in the powerful creators of humanity
And I believe in me
since I know that there are some
who love me

—*Translation by Carlos Amantea
and Renato Valenzuela*

## THE VIVISECTION MAMBO

When she takes the sword, kisses the blade
    just so
And places it gently in my gut and slides it up:
I think on the lace she wears to the dance,
      And before her, breasts like great engines
      Pushing love around the ball, into all of us.

She does bite the blade, doesn't she? By my
White god I miss her, and her thighs lurking
    there
At the edge of my taste, the knowledge that she
In her ripe estates of lavender could so easily
Abandon those of us who love her god knows
Forever, a great streaming out forever.
      She pushes love around the floor, ruffling
      the panes.
      What in god's sweet name can she possibly
      mean?

The sight of those whale bones rising straight up
Out of the chenille, the blasted suns rising up,
Dromedaries lurching out of the morning desert:
      Somehow this has a meaning for me.

She and I were once together in this very
    pyramid.
I was willing to die for the two-eyed moonstone.

The taste of her webbing, tying me to her;
There was something important going on (I
    swear)
Between me and her and the gods,
    Arms wrapped about galaxy arms
    Great legs about god's great legs.

You and I lie in the wallow of such memories:
Sweet clover, acrid perfume, strokes long gone,
Drooping cat's eyes, fallen stars, and her dying.
Thoughts are white buzzards that come to peck
    at me
At times like this, pester me as if I were
    perfect.
    Too much love laid up
    Too long ago, my goddess gone now
    god damn it gone.

—*P.J. Weise*

The Ladies of the School
Of Bliss have announced that each evening
They are preparing to crush thyme
Against their hearts. The hot waxy juices
Will result in something that's to be known as
The Fat Solution For Dying Stars,
(So named after Susie Star or Susie Dying).
Logs (or legs) will be counted up as they turn
Manfully to eat up the wimps like Arthur Q.
Freud, son of the master.

The Ladies of the School of Bliss
Have announced that each evening
In order to save them,
They are preparing to crush thyme
Against the Dying Stars.

—*Lolita Lark*

## Saint Peter got Smashed

Here's to my index—
How many times have I stroked you
(How many times have you stroked me!)
You a constant, and
A pointed friend.

Here's to this old digit named Peter
(As in Peter, Paul, John, Matthew
And Mary Magdalene, she Ms Thumb).
As you can see, I hold my digits
In reverence—and he (or she)
I trust holds me in equal
(and loving)
awe.

Once I smashed Peter with a flathead
Hammer. It's not that we were at war,
It's more that I was drunk, and my friend
Was holding the nail (I was hanging a rail
To cross the skylight, to hold the Lives).
There was blood. "Poor Peter," I said.
I assured him I didn't mean it at all.
The Four Horsemen from the other side,
Those who wielded the instrument of
Such pain, held him, I believe,
In pity and in love.

"It was just a mistake," I say now, but
Ever since then, his visage (looking at me
From under the shield) has seemed darker,
A cloud hanging over the gibbous moon—
Separating me from an old friend,
One who, in days past, was always,
Cocksuredly pointing the way for me.

*—T. K. Müller*

## A Story
## (A Wonderful Story)

Here's a wonderful story. The famous conductor,
Arturo Toscanini once received a letter from a gentleman
living in the mountains of Montana. "Dear Mr. Toscanini,
I listen to your broadcasts every Sunday night on the
radio. I am an old man and I live alone with only my flock
of sheep and my violin in a cabin high above Thompson
Falls. It's been a long winter. The batteries to my radio
are dying and my violin is out of tune. I wonder if you
would be kind enough to strike the note of A next week
so that when I won't be able to hear you any longer, I can
play my violin until the Spring thaw when I can get to
town again."

During the following week's broadcast, Toscanini interrupted his program to say, "I'd like to address the gentleman who wrote me from Montana recently. Here sir is the note of A." That night millions of people heard the note sounded in New York City vibrate across America to a small cabin in Montana where the old shepherd, sitting by his radio, couldn't refrain from fiddling with himself long enough to reach for the violin next to him. He spent the rest of that winter humming along to the sound of salt settling in its shaker.

*—Charles Wing Krafft*

## Fly Love Poem

This morning, at approximately ten forty-two
Immediately after my love & I had come
Up together out of the sea like behemoths—
His back scratched with passionate
Barnacles—he my sweet god's love of ages
        Calls me a "bloodsucking witch."

I swear to you, he lies out side me
Purblind piebald worm gone dead
And dumb—paisley sheets littered,
Dark with 500,000 of his shrimpseed,
Face pale the face of poached scrod:
And he gives forth with a listless litany,
Terminating in piscean spouts of
        "Selfish." "Blood." "Sucking." "Witch."

Over the hemisphere of our rumpled bed,
Nine (count them) nine flies circle constantly:
A minute mosca imbroglio. I carefully consider
Their fat yellow-brown thoraxes filled with
Ugly juices; watch the blue-grey whorl
Of their wings: ceaseless, hopeless—
        The endless rotation of
                Ceaseless, hopeless beasts.

Some flies, I find, are more cantankerous
Than others: mixing freely with their fellows
Like anger at smoke rising from our cigarettes.
Some are more—how shall I say it?—
Of a more pragmatic, phlegmatic turn.
One laggard gets wrangled in those far
Dark, pasty, disgusting hairs—
Then he rejoins the threnody
  At their eleven a.m.
    Sargasso rounds.

Passionless fishbodies turn in oceans, *nu?*
The sour smell of seajuice taken captive by
Kidnapping: the hostage in foreign waters.
Some few loves can, perhaps, be saved
From this Dead Sea. Others, I'm sure,
Turn up like shells from the dark
  Dry circlings in the sand.

    *—The Estate of L. L. Seamans*

### Casida de la Muchacha Dorada

La muchacha dorada
se bañaba en la agua
y el agua se doraba.

Las algas y las ramas
en sombra la asombraban
y el ruiseñor cantaba
por la muchacha blanca.

Vino la noche clara,
turbia de plata mala
con peladas montañas
bajo la brisa parda.

La muchacha mojada
era blanca en el agua
y el agua, llamarada.

Vino el alba sin mancha,
con mil caras de vaca
yerta y amortajada
con heladas guimaldas.

La muchacha de lágrimas
se bañaba entre llamas,
y el ruiseñor lloraba
con las alas quemadas.

La muchacha dorada
era una blanca garza
y el agua la doraba.

*—Federico García-Lorca*

## The Song of the Girl of Gold

The girl of gold
bathed in the water
and the water turned to gold.

Reflections of algae
and branches shadowed her
and the nightingale sang
for the girl of white.

The clear night came,
troubled by evil silver,
dying mountains
under the dark breeze.

The girl, wet,
was white in the water
and the water was in flames.

The dawn came without stain
with a thousand faces of the calf
rigid, and enshrouded
with garlands of ice.

The girl of tears
washed herself between the flames
and the nightingale wept
with burning wings.

The girl of gold
was a white heron
and the water turned her to gold.

*—Translation by Carlos Amantea*

## La Mano de Onan se Queja

Yo soy el sexo de los condenados.
No el jugete de alcoba que economiza vida.
Yo soy la amante de los que no amaron.
Yo soy la esposa de los miserables.
Soy el minuto antes del suicida.
Sola de amor, mas nunca solitaria,
limitada de piel, saco raíces...
Se me llenan de ángeles los dedos,
se me llenan de sexos no tocados.
Me parezco al silencio de los héroes.
No trabajo con carne solamente...
Va más allá de digital mi oficio.
En mi labor hay un obrero alto...
Un Quijote se ahoga entre mis dedos,
una novia también que no se tuvo.
Yo apenas soy violenta intermediaria,
porque también hay verso en mis temblores,
sonrisas que se cuajan en mi tacto,
misas que se derriten sin iglesias,
discursos fracasados que resbalan,
besos que bajan desde el cráneo a un dedo,
toda la tierra suave en un instante.

Es me carne que huye de mi carne;
horizontes que saco de una gota,
una gota que junta

todas los ríos en mi piel, borrachos;
un goterán que trae
todas las aguas de un ciclón oculto,
todas las venas que prisión dejaron
y suben con un viento de licores
a mojarse de abismo en cada uña,
a sacarme la vida de mi muerte.

*—Manuel del Cabral*

## Song to Onan's Complaining Hand

I am the passion of the condemned.
Not the bedroom game that makes lives.
I am the lover of those who didn't love.
I am the wife of *les misérables.*
I am the moment before suicide.
Only of love, but never alone;
limited by skin, I pull out roots...
Multitudes of angels fill my fingers,
fill me with untouchable passion.
I'm the silence of heroes.
My work is not mere flesh...
It goes beyond the digit of my craft.
In my labor there is a higher art,
A Quixote drowned between my fingers,
a lover I never had.

I'm hardly a violent middleman,
for there are also poems in these shakings,
smiles that come together with my touch,
holy masses that melt without churches,
failed speeches that slip away,
kisses that fall from cranium to finger,
all the earth soft, in an instant.

It's my flesh that escapes from my flesh;
horizons pulled out of a single drop,
a drop that joins
all the rivers in my drunken skin;
a huge drop that brings
all the waters of a dark hurricane,
all the inspirations that left prison
and floated up in a drunken wind
to wet themselves in the root of each fingernail,
to take the life of my own death.

*—Translation by Carlos Amantea*
*and Renato Valenzuela*

## Eulogy on the Death of Dickie Dickinson
### (Who Weighed in at 335 Pounds)

If you think Dickie had piggy eyes
You should have known his family—
Made up of gods eating boulders
Plumbed on the very verge of the forest.

Dickie (and his equally seized brother Angie)
Were the original gloomy gods of chance—
Eating, for snacks, a thousand tons or so of
Victorian lace panties, and, for dessert,
An entire platoon of silky parachutes:
Sweets billowing in and out like clouds.

It was a long and desperate war of attrition:
Shoulder attacking haunch, overwhelming thighs,
Pillow arms stacked atop pillow legs
And that tiny fishhead of love nestled somewhere
There among the buns and dozen or so
Bedimpled thighs of white marble veins of basalt.

There was nothing outside the sounds of naked love
To describe the flap of this fat fornication,
The rich fat yellowed sauces of desire dribbling away.
And, all the while, hidden in the folds of their tums
Lived trolls and fairies, demigods out of the Black Forest,
Filling testicles with their puffed-up cries of hunger.

Faced with such roly-poly gods, our own passions
Turned inside out, screwed up like hot trombones;
Our hidden eyes dripped great golden honey-rolls,
Flesh captured itself in mountains of hunger
Volcano-bowls of sadness were left under the plumes.

A mammal's age now stretches the rivers between us.
Eyes huge as white stones roll the faults.
What's left of the nights eats into our days
(And our nightmares).
Fat (not fate)
explains why
you and I
are here
At all.

## The Stars®Us

If you go out there, they say, some quad
rillion dodecathillion miles over
there [pointing] you would find
a corner of the universe where
there is no light no star no
no white no blue no nothing
no, nothing. No, they say
[pointing] nothing. It's very dark.

If we journey there, you and I,
together—we could find a corner
of the universe out of every
star's way where we could see
no north no south no east no west
nothing by nothing do west nothing
(save you)
see nothing
(save you),
nothing
(save you)
(and me).

In that all over darkness
we could be left perfectly
forever (forever) to explore
every corner of you (me), and me (you)
without any people or beasts
(or stars, for that matter)
to offer suggestions, alter

ations
alter
cations
agitations.
So that we (you and me) could grad
ually transform ourselves into the uni
versal trans
formed
bi
polar
i
za
tion
trans
 uni
  ver
   sal
   love
  space
station.

We would pass on 500,000,000 or so quarks,
merging into 500,000,000,000 or so
blue giant white dwarf alpha
zeta eternal macro love-yous:
merging into dark mirrorspace
dark soul all souls night in plu
perfect darkness there where

in the last pass of the uni
verse we pass
all under
 standing
  to merge
   in a new
    macro
    mega
   meta
uni
 verse:
   the two of us
    together the two
     of us we two
    at the beginning
   here at the begin
 here at the be
here at wee too
 weee
  begin
   again
    weeeeee

                              —*Peter Dodge*

## Moon Dog Song

I was out tonight, pissing on the moon
The yellow full moon. The man across the way
Was picking up dogshit with a shovel
Stuffing it into a Safeway bag.

Venus is in bloom tonight.
There are a thousand or so comets
Leaching across the southern sky.
I pretend that they are friends visiting
From Antares coming to visit me
Coming to visit me
To visit me with love
From the cold and wandering star
They call Antares.

Childhood is such a nightmare.
We free ourselves from such nightmares
That came up in darkness; I lay me down
Among silver chords, a dream of spiders
Bagged together clawing their way across
Dark and crowded stairs crawling up...

I have nothing against the man across the way,
With his cleanliness, and his dogs,
And his collection of dogshit.
I have nothing against him
And he, I trust, has nothing against me
And my frozen moment of darkness
Coming up the stairs.
I do not blame him.

Once, when we were too young by far,
You and I stayed up all night,
Beastly drunk on a train to Madrid,
Our lips blood red from blood wine
The night hills like spooks wheeling away.
Drunk blind stupid on *tinto* you my god
Smelling like the lillies-of-the-valley
Wound into me as we beat down
The dark tracks to Madrid;
You over me I said no no no
Not that way you said they don't mind
*Malrincones* like us making love
In a very public private way
I said no no I said no please
No not not that way no
      Not please without you again.

I was out tonight, pissing on the moon.
It's no different now, now that the beast
That worried you and me died on the tracks
Outside Madrid, run over an eon or so ago.
It's now no different: you saying nothing
      you smelling the dead lilies,
        looking at the dead light,
          and all over me the child webs
          coming up at me again.

*—Ángel Pérez*

## Song to Supp-Hose

I remember you and me on a highway
To somewhere. The shadows had turned
To fool's gold; there was a white buzzard
Crying above us. You sideeyed me
And said, *They gave us the script, but they*
*Forgot to tell us the plot line—and they*
*Still refuse to tell us who the author is.*

I recall your mother, hands spidered in time,
Ankles swathed in fat, saying, at least 1,000
    times
"I'm tired of people telling me what's good for
    me."
Then she would nod, dewlaps waggling,
Her face touched by nets, eyes blind by moons.

Sometimes I think it gets too late too soon;
And sometimes I think we're too good to die.

Love, and the flowers, and your whimsy
Is hard to forget—no matter how I try.
They've made us into wise gods (I think)
But flies and spiders are tangling our days.

Love, and the ages,
And time comes on
Like a ragged shawl:
Sometimes I think it gets
Too late too early,
And sometimes I think
They should have
Strangled us alive
In the crib.

*—P. V. Astor, III*

## The Return of Der Führer

Adolf Hitler has returned to earth again, you
     know—
Revivified by The Divine to journey amongst us
     again.
Most have not yet heard of this personal re-
     armageddon,
Have no idea that this slight corporal, one of
     god's agents,
Is now intimately involved with the dark but
     needy natives
Of the Mongu area near the Zambeze River.

Der Fuhrer has returned as a crab *(Phthirius
     pubis)*
On this the first of 1,000,000,000 scheduled
     visits.
He is also to return, they say, as one or more
Stinkbugs, chinchbugs, bedbugs, potato bugs,
Lightbugs, darkbugs, *pediculus humanus,
     drosophila,*
Carp weevils and jigger fleas, each visit being
The first of a billion of a billion
Of a billion-billion.

I hear there are a few other bodies floating
     about
Other floating solar systems that are expecting
     him

Sometime in the next hecto-millennia for
    additional
Giga-reruns of his various bugheaded
    reincarnations.
They are not anticipating nor not not
anticipating
His presence (they never do)
            They
                are
            just waiting.

When Der Führer returned to earth for the
        next previous go-round
(In South America, shortly after his departure
        from the bunker
In the spring of 1945)
He came back as a nematode. They say he pulled
        himself up
A mighty two mm., waved his feelers, and gave
        a stirring speech
In buggy language to the massed midges in a
        towering field of pigweed.
Taking heart from his reception, Der Führer
        invaded
The springtime jute harvest just outside La
        Sangre de María,
And then attempted to incite a purge of katydids
        in a field of milpa.

Finally, they tell us he successfully incited a
        revolt of chiggers
Near the peasant huts twenty-five miles west
        of Puerto Ángel.

Adolf Hitler, in this most recent of his returns,
Was finally terminated,
Squeezed to death between thumb and
        forefinger
(Left a mere smear of grey-green corpuscles)
At the hands of a crippled wall-eyed peasant
Named Ignacio El Triste:
A man who truly had no knowledge of the
        stature of his visitor.

They say Hitler has yet to divine the purpose
        of the divine,
And his particular place in the order of divine
        things.
They also say he has not lost his need nor flair
        for leadership
And a colony of pinworms are looking forward
To his apprenticeship in their pain-in-the-ass
        fraternity
                Amongst the dark spirals of man
                (And woman)
                Kind.

                                —J. W. Torg

# Jesus Under Water

I've been told that Jesus came on a dung-colored
    mule
His beard moving in the wind a bloody rose
His feet dripping on the thighs of a mule
    They called "Agnes Dei."

They say his eyes were clouded like the wind
That beat across the Kyzyl Kum Desert;
They say that if you listened closely,
You could hear his heart beat and beat and stop
    Like the wind
    Across the desert.

They say that god's juices ran like tears
From the nine famous exits (wept like the sunset);
He rode the dung-colored mule, his head hung down,
And he brooded mightily over the usual paradoxes:
    "If I am here, why am I here?"
And
    "Is my mule a divine?"
And
    "Who was I before I was?"
And, most of all,
    "Why can't they stop killing each other
    In the name of the name
    (In the name of god
    Why can't they stop?)"
They say (I think) that Jesus left this earth
Riding on the back of a gold-and-ivory lion
A cruel beast that snarled at the penitents

Along the road to The Hill of Sorrows.
The blood of his brow laced the beast's gold
    mane,
His body curved like the waters of the Tigris.

He left our domain (they swear by their faith)
On the back of a winged lion
Out of the sands of the Great Atacama
    Where the wind blows
    And the sun has finally,
    For all good time, descended.

The next day (they say) they found him
Spinning at the mouth of the river.
The natives in their divine simplicity now
Worship the waters as god. They give over their
    ashes,
To the sacred river they refer to as
The Sign Of God's Good Grace.
    That's where they found
    What was left of his bones
    Turning round like hands reaching
    Turning like hands reaching out.

*—Al Hefid*

## Did you See?
## She had Flowers up Her Nose

Did you see the flowers up her nose?
If you had seen where she had gazed,
If you had seen her eyes turn again,
If you had seen the lust of her, the swallows
And the graze of the dying flowers—
I think you might have been touched.

They had planned to leave her but one grey lily,
A lily to eat at her breast. They put, as well,
A twisted oak to grow out her sodden soul.
That's what the gardeners had planned, they say.

But I tell you, women like this
Have cracked before. Some do it slowly,
In tiny plots. Some all at once,
Taking whole fields with them.
She tried them all.
She had been sent
To test us with small acts of
Madness,
Or kindness,
Or both.
She put flowers there to show us
What we had become.

*—Emma St. James*

## Loos

They took my boy to Loos.
He smelled of leather.
He died there in Loos
In trenches, of lead (they say).
They decorated the lads
Most dreadfully.

No one was there to bless him.
Teeth turned seeds to bloom,
Eyes to roots, a grey below innocence
In the field they call
Passchendaele.
Which means,
I hear,
"Still in bloom."

You don't know the gods at the Somme:
They pluck off buds like moons;
Pale creatures turn fat and still,
Swell up and burst like ballons;
Nights are noisy with the charge of sepulchres.

When they took him away, I thought
I heard him wail; now he's down there
Making caissons out of poppies,
The boy we carved out of heaven's breath,
A boy with the powder of love.
Now just a breath of lead, smell of steel.

## SONG OF THE FORGET-ME-NOT

Now I look at the garden,
At the garden. They say I had
A green thumb. Now it grows like
The bittersweet vine, this way
and that, on a bed of bracken.

I used to go out to the garden,
The birds and I in the garden.
The word "cystic" has a garden
Of meanings. Can you smell
The peppermint, the basil,
     the marjoram?

          Mother said
I must have done something
Wrong in another life. Did I hurt
Some babe a thousand years ago?
She said I didn't love Jesus enough,
Did I hurt Jesus two thousand years ago?
Pray enough, she says. I pray now,
I pray now and my prayers wind
     like maidenhair.
         Fibrosis.

Daddy says I once had a nice body, bewitching eyes.
There are mockingbirds in the boxwood below
The forget-me-not. I once lay on the earth
Smelling the earth, the wild oats, the moon
    blossom, a passion flower. Did I do wrong,
To love the earth so? I used to go out,
                    To the Garden.

—*Cynthia Weiss*

# Sing Ho! To the New Keyboard

Now is the time
(Sing ho!) now is
The time, they say,
For love, my love. Now
Is the time for all good
Men of love to come
(Love-to-come!)
To the aid of their partly.

Did you say partly?

Partly yes. For all good men
Abound around and found that
Now is the time for all of them
To come to the air of their love.
Partly.

Air? Partly. Good men come
With an air to their partlies
Of the first part. Fart.
Do you know that those who know
They know know not that
Now is the time for those
Who know the nose now
To come to those who
Know not that they know
Not at all! Partly. (Ah-choo!)

                                    —*A. W. Allworthy*

# January 1940

*Roy Fuller wrote the perfect apothegm for all
who might choose to become Poets.
We dedicate this book to him—and this poem to them.*

Swift had pains in his head.
Johnson dying in bed
Tapped the dropsy himself.
Blake saw a flea and an elf.
Tennyson could hear the shriek
Of a bat. Pope was a freak.
Emily Dickinson stayed
Indoors for a decade.
Water inflated the belly
Of Hart Crane, and of Shelley.
Coleridge was a dope.
Southwell died on a rope.
Byron had a round white foot.
Smart and Cowper were put
Away. Lawrence was a fidget.
Keats was a midget.
Donne, alive in his shroud,
Shakespeare in the coil of a cloud,
Saw death as he
Came crab-wise, dark and massy.
I envy not only their talents
And fertile lack of balance
But the appearance of choice
In their sad and fatal voice.

# LIST OF AUTHORS

A. W. Allworthy ..................... *60*

Carlos Amantea ................. *20, 33, 35*

P. V. Astor, III ..................... *49*

T. F. Bierly ......................... *22*

Manuel del Cabra .................... *38*

Jeremy D. Colon ..................... *47*

Peter Dodge ........................ *44*

Anwak Fayoumi ...................... *13*

G. J. Fogerty ....................... *42*

Roy Fuller ......................... *61*

Federico García-Lorca ............... *36*

Al Hefid ........................... *54*

Charles Wing Krafft ................. *32*

Edna J. Lacey ...................... *57*

Lolita Lark ........................ *29*

P. P. McFeelie ...................... *9*

Brook Morris, Jr .................... *20*

Pater Müller ....................... *30*

Aquiles Nazoa ...................... *25*

Alexander A Potebnja ................ *11*

Emma St. James ..................... *56*

Ignacio Schwartz ................... *17*

Leslie Seamans ..................... *34*

Jeremy W. Torg ..................... *51*

Renato Valenzuela ................. *25, 38*

P. J. Weise ........................ *27*

Cynthia Weiss ...................... *58*

# INDEX TO FIRST LINES

Adolf Hitler has returned to earth again . . . . . . . . . . . . . . . . . . . . . . . . 51

All the babies were behaving as if they were moons . . . . . . . . . . . . . . . . . . . 20

April is the cruellest month, breeding . . . . . . . . . . . . . . . . . . . . . . . . . . . 9

*Arma virumque cano, Troiae qui primus ab oris* . . . . . . . . . . . . . . . . . . . . . . 83

*Creo en Pablo Neruda, todopoderoso* . . . . . . . . . . . . . . . . . . . . . . . . . . . . 23

Darling there is a worm in your flower . . . . . . . . . . . . . . . . . . . . . . . . . . . 19

Did you see the flowers up her nose? . . . . . . . . . . . . . . . . . . . . . . . . . . . . 56

Flow gently, sweet Afton, among thy green braes . . . . . . . . . . . . . . . . . . . . 81

Here's a wonderful story . . . . . . . . . . . . . . . . . . . . . . . . . . . . . . . . . . . . 32

Here's to my index . . . . . . . . . . . . . . . . . . . . . . . . . . . . . . . . . . . . . . . . 30

I am the passion of the condemned . . . . . . . . . . . . . . . . . . . . . . . . . . . . . 40

I believe in Pablo Neruda, almighty creator of heaven and earth . . . . . . . . . . .25

I could hear the border guards cheering . . . . . . . . . . . . . . . . . . . . . . . . . . 17

If you go out there, they say, some quadrillion . . . . . . . . . . . . . . . . . . . . . . 44

If you think Dickie had piggy eyes . . . . . . . . . . . . . . . . . . . . . . . . . . . . . . 42

I remember you and me on a highway . . . . . . . . . . . . . . . . . . . . . . . . . . . . 49

I've been told that Jesus came on a dung-colored mule . . . . . . . . . . . . . . . . . 54

I was out tonight, pissing on the moon . . . . . . . . . . . . . . . . . . . . . . . . . . . 47

*La muchacha dorada* . . . . . . . . . . . . . . . . . . . . . . . . . . . . . . . . . . . . . . 36

Let us go then, you and I . . . . . . . . . . . . . . . . . . . . . . . . . . . . . . . . . . . 100

My family laughs before the fire . . . . . . . . . . . . . . . . . . . . . . . . . . . . . . . 22

My mother groan'd, my father wept . . . . . . . . . . . . . . . . . . . . . . . . . . . . . 16

*Nel mezzo del cammin di nostra vita* . . . . . . . . . . . . . . . . . . . . . . . . . . . . 88

Now I look at the garden . . . . . . . . . . . . . . . . . . . . . . . . . . . . . . . . . . . . 58

Now is the time (Sing ho!) now is . . . . . . . . . . . . . . . . . . . . . . . . . . . . . . .60

Of man's first disobedience, and the fruit . . . . . . . . . . . . . . . . . . . . . . . . . 15

Swift had pains in his head . . . . . . . . . . . . . . . . . . . . . . . . . . . . . . . . . . 61

The curfew tolls the knell of parting day . . . . . . . . . . . . . . . . . . . . . . . . . . 77

The girl of gold . . . . . . . . . . . . . . . . . . . . . . . . . . . . . . . . . . . . . . . . . . 37

The Ladies of the School . . . . . . . . . . . . . . . . . . . . . . . . . . . . . . . . . . . . 29

The poetry of earth is never dead . . . . . . . . . . . . . . . . . . . . . . . . . . . . . . . 97

The woods decay, the woods decay and fall . . . . . . . . . . . . . . . . . . . . . . . . . 9

The wrath of Peleus' son, the direful spring . . . . . . . . . . . . . . . . . . . . . . . . 85

This morning, at approximately ten forty-two . . . . . . . . . . . . . . . . . . . . . . . 34

They took my boy to Loos . . . . . . . . . . . . . . . . . . . . . . . . . . . . . . . . . . . . 57

Whan that Aprille with hise shoures sote . . . . . . . . . . . . . . . . . . . . . . . . . 104

When she takes the sword, kisses the blade just so . . . . . . . . . . . . . . . . . . . 27

*Yo soy el sexo de los condenados* . . . . . . . . . . . . . . . . . . . . . . . . . . . . . . . 38

Youthful folly has success . . . . . . . . . . . . . . . . . . . . . . . . . . . . . . . . . . . 13

# BIOGRAPHICAL NOTES

Douglas Cruickshank was born in California. Over the years, he has found himself attracted to photography, birds, bees, large butterflies, very large words, and very, very large dogs. His sheep, Lambchop, was awarded the 1965 Grand Champion ribbon at the local County Fair in the Range Ewe division. Cruickshank studied filmmaking at the CIA. His writing appears in *Salon, The San Francisco Examiner Magazine,* and *RALPH.*

Lolita Lark was born in the Middle West, one of the members of the Trapp family. She grew up in New England, and travelled extensively as a teenager. After a near-death experience in the Northwest at the age of eighteen, she became a Zoroastrian, and later married a Swiss linguist, Hermann Lark. She has translated several works of Schiller, including *An die Freude.*

Lorenzo W. Milam was born in Florida. He helped start several non-commercial radio stations, was publisher of *The Fessenden Review,* and has written books on travel, disability, family therapy, and communications. Articles of his have appeared in *The Washington Post, The San Francisco Chronicle, The Los Angeles Times, The St. Louis Post-Dispatch, The Vancouver Sun, The Whole Earth Review* and *The Utne Reader.*